CLOAKS

OF

MINISTRY

DEBORAH J JOHNSON

SISTA LLC, 1712 6TH Ave STE 100 PMB 1155

Tacoma, Washington 98405. Coachs2@proton.me

ALL SCRIPTURE QUOTATIONS ARE TAKEN FROM THE KING JAMES VERSION OF THE HOLY BIBLE - STANDARD EDITION UNLESS OTHERWISE NOTED. (1930/2013),

AN APPLICATION HAS BEEN SUBMITTED TO THE LIBRARY OF CONGRESS. PRINTED BY: KDP (KINDLE DIRECT PUBLISHING) USA

FOREWARD

The father of the righteous shall greatly *rejoice: and he that begetteth a wise child shall have joy of him."*
Proverbs 23:24

From a counselor's and personal perspective, Cloakes of Ministry was a joy to edit and preview. DJ is a true mentor and woman of God! I felt a mantle being passed on to *me as I read and received the conviction of the Lord through the* impartation *of yoke*-breaking, healing, and truth being released. This is a time of great deception under the spirit of this age, in which there is abundant twisting of the truth-right is wrong and wrong is right, life is about pleasure over godly living, et cetera. I have been blessed and convicted simultaneously via the text. It is a must read for-everyday people, clergy, mentors, and leaders for sure! Please get a copy and urge others to do the same…

Phadria Reed,

AAS, AAT, BSW, MED,

LMFT, LCDC,NCC, PLPC

DEDICATION

Most of all I give special dedication of this book to (God) who gave me the foresight and wisdom to write it for the encouragement and knowledge of His people.

****

I also give dedication to my former Pastors and Generals in the faith that have gone on who taught me a lot about the foundation of ministry, how to get closer to God, and what a good Pastor and Leader looks like. (Pastor Willie C. Vaughan Jr, Bishop Vernon Richardson, and Apostle John H. Boyd, Sr.)

GRATITUDE

Much "Thanks" to my children, Leonard Jackson & Shamiesha Ebothemen for their support, and encouragement in the writing of this book. I will forever be grateful for your belief in me and diligence towards my crazy thoughts and works of this book. I pray that it will be an encouragement and a benefit to many as it may answer questions of those who are inquisitive like me.

I am truly grateful God brought you into my life and gave me the opportunity to be a part of yours. Thank You for helping me realize who I am. (For as you love me I dedicate my love back to you.)

* Remember whenever life hits you with a sling shot, bounce back and fly*.

Love You

ACKNOWLEDGMENT

To my amazing **"SISTAS"**

(Phadria Reed, Darlene Keyes, and Trudy Hughley), along with other friends and clergy that pushed and supported me in this endeavor. Words cannot express my gratitude of how much I appreciate you. May God continue to bless you and yours.

TABLE OF CONTENTS

Introduction

God is building up and establishing the church. Some of the things that went on before cannot be carried over into the new church and leaders that dominated previously will not continue to dominate any more. The saying, “Come as you are,” has become the saying of “What qualifies you to be here?” The focus seems to be on how much money can you give, while the pure essence of the church has vanished. The innocence of the lamb has been buried, and a darkness of “What can you do for me lately?” has appeared to take over. Therefore, one could ask is the way to the altar become a thing of the past, and has a season of hypocrisy taken over?

In society today it seems the attitude of gratitude has turned into an attitude of manipulation. Either you do what I say, or you are in disobedience, and you’re going straight to hell. The standards of doctrines have been raised at the cost of taking each other down for the slightest mistake one makes, while the world is looking on watching the fiasco of Christians taring each other down. Prayer seems to be a foreign word and gossip seems to be the key. Some say their doctrine is better than the others, their doctrine is the right way to go, and if you don’t believe what we believe, or in what we say, there’s no place for you in heaven, because we don’t see where you fit in.

The purpose of this book is to bring awareness to some of the things occurring behind the scenes of ministry. It is not to condemn or make mockery but to engage those involved to correct their behavior. It is also to encourage those who have experienced abuse not to be silent, but to become stronger, to move forward and overcome their situations.

People are looking and searching for "Hope", and one can only ask can the church at this time provide them with the "Comfort" and "Hope" so greatly needed? I invite you to come walk with us through this journey, and hopefully you will see this powerful revelation for change.

Prophetess Deborah J Johnson writes this book under the unction of the Holy Spirit to bring awareness to some of the things we as leaders do in the church to deter people from following after the heart of God. This book is written to help leaders to be watchful and aware of how their behavior affects others in their decision making and their reactions towards their family in the future. Hidden things can harm more than help, and people need to speak up when they encounter or see abusive situations. *(For the church is here to help heal the broken and wounded heart, not to destroy it's very existence)*

CHAPTER 1

DISCREET SINS

CHAPTER 1

DISCREET SINS

In your day to day encounters what do you value most, your thoughts, your emotions or your heart?

"You cannot lead others until you have first learned to lead yourself." (Dharma, 2022) There are very many discreet relations going on in the church today. Some are through fear, manipulation, via clicks and groups, things done in secret privately or in public to control and manipulate a person or persons. There are those who focus on what one has to offer, and what they can do for them. Lust and sexual favors is a definite wave that is encouraged and manipulation of the heart is a two-fold stage. For the ones they trusted the most appear to be the ones that harm the most. Instead of encouraging the flock to come to Jesus, they appear to be encouraging their own ways causing low-self esteem, and guilt in the hearts of many which leads them astray. Families are being taken advantage of, husbands and wives are being split up by deceitful leaders, who instead of praying through their situation are taking advantage of those involved. Some single people find themselves in compromising situations where they become victims of the leaderships games they play. False prophecies are a part of these deeds, lies, intimidation, and rejection.

People are searching for a better way of life and finding out that some leaders in ministry are similar to prowlers in the street preying on the vulnerable who don't know any better. Leaders who they hold in high esteem let them down by making sexual moves, lusting after them in their vulnerable states, and displaying jealousy over their gifts, and knowledge. Leaders at times date knowing they have no marital intentions, and some leaders prey on children, yet they remain in position to continue on to their next prey. Discreet sins describes what the Bible states in (Jeremiah 17:9, KJV) *"The heart is deceitful above all things, And desperately wicked; Who can know it?"*

In a recent study by Life Way Christian Resources, 1 in 10 young Protestants have left the church due to sexual misconduct. Several churchgoers ages 18 to 34 and some older generations have experienced sexual harassment, and are afraid to attend church. The research found the high risk groups are ages 12 to 34, and whereas, some of the older generation tolerated the sexual harassment, younger generations are not. (Shell nut, 2019). *The following are episodes of abuse in ministry and the church:*

According to the U. S. Bishop " Charter for the Protection of Children and Young People" more than 4,200 allegations of sexual abuse of minors by catholic clergy and others were reported ending June 30, 2020. (2021, Catholic News Service). The report findings stated 2,455 priests, 31 deacons, & 282 unknown clergy were involved in these abuse cases where 195 out of 197 dioceses and eparchies participated in the audit. Archbishop Gomez mentioned in the annual report regarding findings and recommendation that : "While we cannot give you back what has been taken from you," "we do commit ourselves to doing everything in our power to help you to heal and to fight the scourge of abuse in the church and in the wider society." (2021, Catholic News Service).

Abuse of sexual scandals in the Southern Baptist Church in 2022 was running so rapidly that it was called an "apocalypse"; meaning an uncovering and disclosure of information or a dispute. The report in the Guardian mentioned hundreds of church leaders were accused or found guilty of abusing children or mistreating survivors. A 205 page document was released naming many Baptist leaders and members. This list included 700 entries in cases between 2000 and 2019. As a result a third-party investigation was released by Guideposts Solutions. The SBC leader Rollan Slade and Willie McLauren stated, "Reminds us of the devastation and destruction brought about by sexual abuse. Our prayer is that the survivors of these heinous acts find hope and healing, and that churches will utilize this list proactively to protect and care for the most vulnerable among us."

350 leaders and volunteers were revealed to be involved in the sexual activities and public accusations. It was found that the executive committee leaders failed the public and the community because they mishandled and mistreated the victims and survivors of the abuse cases. It was also found that the SBC general counsel and spokesman kept their own secret list of abusive ministers who they had accusations of for decades which they were trying to cover up and protect the pastors along with the SBC from liability.(2022, Helmore).

Many victims were stonewalled; ignored, blocked, and never given a response to their allegations. Most were disbelieved, met with refrain or no action was taken. This meant the molestation continued and remained covered up while most of the pastors stayed in their positions and the congregation never knew about it because it was not investigated.

Per author Anthea Butler another form of abuse in the SBC is called "critical race theory" which some say is still prevalent today where there is 14% African American Christians and 85% identify as white in the Southern Baptist Church organization. (2022, Helmore). A lot of the African American Christian leaders and evangelicals left due to the following statement used by the organization:“the gospel of Jesus Christ alone grants the power to change people and society.”

The New Republic said this statement obscured the reality of racial history in the U. S. This caused racial terror which still goes on today where emancipated blacks were denied rights to vote and was covered up by the church along with the sexual abuse.” (2022, Helmore).

Sexual abuse took place in Brooklyn’s Progressive Baptist Church of Brownsville. The pastor was accused of rape of his own daughter between the age of 9 and 14years old after her mother passed away. Some members stated this was something that happened often in the church, and they were tired of it happening and feeling hopeless. Per M L Sampson a member of the church who stated “Sexual abuse is a disruption of child play, child innocence, child freedom, child imagination, and child relationship to God and others.”

In the U. S. 10% of all children experience some form of sexual abuse. 18.75% are girls before they reach ages 14 and 17, and some are younger. Child marriage is common among Black people in the U.S. compared to other groups. Some girls are forced to do this by their church. An example of this is Sherry Johnson who was raped and forced to marry her rapist.

At Denton Bible Church in North Texas a youth pastor sexually abused 14 girls in two different churches. There were many red flags but the leaders ignored it and were more focused on covering up the abuse. This abuse happened in the late 90's and it was exposed in 2005. The leaders were warned several times, yet the abuser was not disciplined, and was recommended for promotion. Currently the abuser is in federal prison with a sentence for sexually assaulting two girls on the church youth trip. (2022, Brown, Fox 4).

A former minister was accused of sex trafficking his preteen daughter in Wilmington, Delaware, (2021, Delaware News Journal).

In Toledo Ohio a pastor groomed a 14 year old teen to have sex with other pastors and ministers after pledging before his congregation he would take care of her. (2019, Associated Press)

Youth Leaving The Church

Cultural Life Research stated "Church pews may be full of teenagers, but a new study says college students might be a much rarer sight on Sunday mornings." LifeWay Research found two-thirds (66 percent) of American young adults who attended a Protestant church regularly for at least a year as a teenager say they also dropped out for at least a year between the ages of 18 and 22.

However, the drop out rate is better than before in 2007. 44% percent attend church now at least twice a month per Scott McConnell, who is the executive director. He says they are seeing more youth come back to the Protestant church than they previously had.

Most young adults stop attending church due to family concerns, going to college, becoming independent, and other personal priorities. However, not all teenagers leave the church. 34% consistently attend twice a month or through age 22. (2019, Earl.)

Young Black youth are dropping out of church for different and cultural reasons than White students. They say according to LifeWay Research that they are "Looking for a church home." It has been stated that less Black young adults are attending church at a lower rate than the elderly. Yet, they feel they are more attached to their home church after leaving. (2019, Banks, LifeWay Research) Some youth saw the church as an important part of their lives, and some wanted a closer relationship with God. 56% wanted the church to guide them, and 43% wanted to follow their parents footsteps. It appears it is good for parents to start taking an interest in youth coming and being a part of the church. Trueblood believes a church should have a strategy and stay focused on keeping the youth in the church and not just when they are children. because this helps to keep them in the church. (2019, Earls, Lifeway Research).

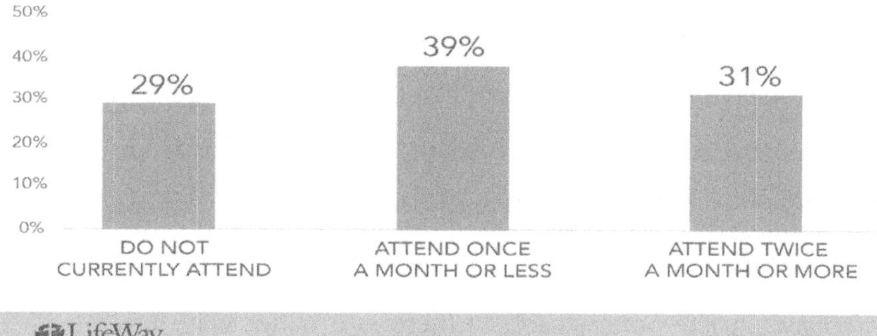

Covered Up Reasons Youth Leave The Church

LifeWay Christian Resources states 10% of Protestant youth under 35 have left the church due to sexual misconduct that was not taken seriously. 9% of the youth stated they stopped going to church because they did not feel safe. (2019, Shellnutt). Youth America was accused by 100 former members and interns of having a pattern of sexual misconduct, mismanagement of funds, and exploitation of minors. A petition was done by more than

3,100 signatures calling for the closure of the Youth America and Church of the Harvest (COTH) It was also stated that the staff and board be held accountable dating back to more than two decades, but it was stated most of the allegations "were false, misleading and hateful".

Interns mentioned they were not paid but had to pay monies for the experience. Some stated there was a lot of mind control. Others have left the church and were too afraid to go up against the church because some received pressure from former members to be silent. (2020, Roys). Overall, it appears a way of manipulation has grasped the heart of many people blocking their way to Christ. Today Christ wants us to see there is a better way in spite of the obstacles that come to hinder and block our view of truth. The true meaning of ministry should engulf clarity, and purity from the heart which includes the love of God, our families, self love, and others. It's not about what you can do for me, what I can get from you, or what qualifies you to serve God.

Abusive behavior can happen in the boardroom, prayer room, finance room, choir room, inside a car, office, or any place where one displays inappropriate behavior. At times some leaders. can make one feel uncomfortable by asking for secret favors, staring at their private areas, and using inappropriate touching. Behaviors such as these can lead to unwanted pregnancy, homosexuality, intimidated companionship, low self-esteem, and spousal abuse.

Mind you, these sins go both ways with men and women. There are women who abuse as well as men. They set up leaders and lie on them, manipulate, and sexually subdue them to have their way with them. They also bring shame to discredit who they are in order for them to fall, and destroy their homes. God is not pleased!

Discreet sins can take on many forms. They are kept as deep dark secrets and ignored such as clergy spousal abuse. There are clergy wives who sit in service and observe their spouse preaching as he interacts with his "baby mamma" and they grin and bear it. Deception behind the cloth of discreet sins can be unbearable for some. One clergy spouse stated. "As he became more powerful he became more rigid, and displayed more emotional dominance in their home with her and their children." (Baird and Gleeson, 2017).

Abuse can happen when the purpose of the other person is not understood or known. Therefore, there is truth in this statement, "Where purpose is not known, abuse is inevitable, and it will not be used appropriately." (Monroe, 2001).

Some pastors who don't like confident women, and desire to see them be submissive, believe a gentle beating is required to keep them in order. (Baird Gleeson, 2017) Others say, "A woman should stay in her place, but they don't realize a woman's place is in God." Nevertheless, it's a blessing when males and females can work together to accomplish what God desires on the earth with no competitiveness, but through mutual respect for each other and love. (Monroe, 2001)

Another form of abuse in ministry is excessive drinking, smoking, addiction, and clubbing. Leaders that engage in this behavior preach from the pulpit that their congregation is going to hell for partaking, yet they partake of these things themselves. (Monroe, 2001). Some engage in adultery, pornography, pedophile behavior, and still remain in their positions with a tap on the hand or they are moved to another position by the church. One thing they forget is that God sees it all, no matter how they try to hide it or cover it up.

Discreet sins is a "worldwide" problem in ministry. Yes, it may come in a subtle way, openly, boldly, through a group or clique discreetly, but overall, it is all SIN. It occurs in every culture, and economic status among males, and females. Some recommendations to handle these situations is the church must find ways to deal with abuse in ministry. Incidentally, "therapy" has been taboo in the church. However, it is very much needed now because the mental health of those who have experienced abuse is greatly at stake. Those who have engaged in this behavior have even more detriment upon their soul. Openness, along with ministry leaders being concerned and dealing with these issues can help with this overdue process. Not addressing the issue is the problem, and ignoring it gives consent. Yes, indeed some may be offended by these issues and concerns. They may even state you are disrespectful for bringing it up or even having a thought about such. However, the fact remains it needs to be addressed, and victims' voices must be heard.

Today many people are indeed searching for answers, and someone to believe in that can bring peace to their souls while on the pathway to truth. The question is can the church offer them the truth they are looking for, and the comfort they need for their troubled souls and minds? The Bible says. “teach them the way of the Lord”, but could one ask as a leader in ministry can they see that truth they search so vigorously for in you? Take a look at your life and ask who am I, and can they see God in me?

In looking for a good leader ask yourself how are they contributing to my life, and do they bring out the best in me? Check to see if they are enhancing your life, or hindering your stride. Continuing to stay in an abusive situation can be devastating to your character, lower your self-esteem, make you bitter, hold you back and damage your soul. However, abuse in ministry is being brought to the forefront because it must be dealt with, and not ignored. Things are changing due to the “People’s Choice”, “Awareness” and “God”.

CHAPTER 2

DECEPTION: THE CHAMELEONS

CHAPTER 2

DECEPTION: THE CHAMELEONS

Who fills the void in your life?

"What once could control and destroy, must now give way to Jesus. Anything meant for evil, Jesus has redeemed." (Drumsta, 2022) The church was set up to be a Legacy of the greatness of God. The Legacy of the Lord lives on and on, from age to age, and is talked about more than anyone or any entity throughout the world. His church was to be a place where the Holy Spirit could dwell, where He felt welcomed, and could dwell among His people. However, today that sacred place somehow has been turned into a den of deception for many deceitful vipers. The Bible says, "*If any man defile the temple of God, him shall God destroy; for the temple of God is holy, which temple ye are."* (1 Corinthians 3:17, KJV)

It appears for some the church has become a "Hall of Fame" for many leaders while the people sit back and watch the stage of actors perform. Indeed as we travel on our journey of life with good intentions in our hearts at times we may meet someone which we call a "Chameleon". In the process of life one may be trying their best to be genuine with God and live the best they can to fulfill their purpose and plans God has for them. Nevertheless, there always seem to be a snare or device in the way just waiting to destroy that dream, or the person in you. That device I am speaking of can be symbolic of the "chameleon", which is a highly specialized word for a "Lizard". It comes in 202 different species and ranges in different colors where they can blend in with their background to create a camouflage making it difficult for anyone to see them.

The chameleon has eyes that move in several directions at the same time, but it's number one enemy is "Man". The chameleon can also lay flat and hiss like a snake if it feels intimidated. Therefore, they can be ready to strike at any time. One must be aware of the "chameleons" setting waiting to deceive and destroy you. Unwittingly, that chameleon may be someone you confided in, a leader or a trusted person in ministry that for one reason or another is plotting to deceive you. When a person has a deceitful heart they become the predator, and you become the bait. People who have a "Chameleon Spirit" like to operate in solitude, behind the scenes, and will put the person on public display to embarrass them. They agree with you one minute, then do just the opposite the next. The chameleon stays in the ear of the leader who lacks clear discernment and brings bad news, lies, or things they can use against someone to cause dissension and create problems. Their competitive spirit turns the views of the leaders against you, when someone else speaks ill of you. The leader then changes their mind, and come up with "Y*ou know I love you right", and stops you cold or acts differently towards you.* The chameleon can shout like the best of saints, prophecy, speak in tongues, and lay hands, yet they have a defiant spirit, and seek to destroy the God in you. One could say they are a hypocrite, but a good hypocrite that takes on many different forms and identities. They can camouflage themselves at any time to make it appear they are very honest and are doing things for your best interest and good, yet all the time they are jealous and despise the very anointing in your life.

One must be aware that the chameleon can be a leader of the flock where people confide and trust in them, yet they are endeavoring to hold them back, and put them under their thumb. The chameleon spirit takes a hold of a person and they display deceitful behavior, where they can change like the wind. If the main leader has no clear discernment they have been deceived. This person walks by sight, not by faith. This person seeks fame, position, acknowledgment, and renown reputation. They lay waiting for the one they want to conquer and control, and plots their demise. They can quietly destroy your personality, your family, your home, your life and ministry if you allow it.

The chameleon is a predator that mimics a person's ministry, their anointing, and is trusted by many. It has to keep up its image so that people don't discover who they really are because they wear a mask, have a hidden identity and a hidden agenda. They prey on the sheep through gaining trust, their vulnerability, misleading them, wickedness, finding loopholes, being overly critical. and doing unnatural things. If one is not careful, they may take away their self-esteem, cause a person to lose their very soul, and take away their breath of life.

The chameleon, the deceptive one, only sees a reflection of who they are and who they want to be while obtaining their goal, no matter what the cost. A person cannot become better than they are, whether they are the leader or not. This person cannot out do them, for they are the one to be looked up to, the one who is to be praised and idolized, not God. Some would call this Godly boasting but it is all about them, not God.

Mind you, at times they do their dirt publicly and consistently apologize: then they repeat the behavior or cycle again showing their brokenness inside, yet not acknowledging being broken at all. Some may say it is evil, but it is real. Leaders with the chameleon spirit don't build up the ones God has placed under them, instead they put them down, shun them, and hide them from those who can help them grow. Therefore, God is exposing the "chameleons" in ministry because the chameleon spirit has advanced and taken some churches in a different direction than what was originally intended. It has become a business, entertainment, a mockery to the standards and word of God, and has blocked the Holy Spirit out. Some places have become a function of control, “my way or the highway”. Some leaders hit their members, ball them out in front of other staff and their families, and abuse them publicly to show whose in charge causing chaos and intimidation in the church. One may ask, "Does God truly dwell there?” The Bible says *“So shall they fear the name of the Lord from the west, and his glory from the rising of the sun. When the enemy shall come in like a flood, the Spirit of the Lord shall lift up a standard against him.”* (Isaiah 59:19, KJV).

God has a Legacy to fulfill, a purpose for the church, and is bringing healing to His children from the inside, out. We are definitely living in a historical moment where God is making Himself known even more throughout the world. For we can find joy and peace within through Him. I urge you to search for your true identity and check out the purpose God has for your life. Stop guessing who you are, and know who you are and to whom you belong. Ask God to destroy that defiant personality and behavior in you. Trust God and stop running from faith to faith trying to get a word. Talk to Him and He will talk to you.

Watch out and be aware of the abusers and deception in ministry. God has shifted the church and you must shift with it, because you are the “Church”. The days are gone where you come to the church to get noticed. It’s time to work together instead of against each other. Time is out for "You're the Man or You're the Woman". One doesn't have to worry about the pastor not speaking to them, or greeting them, because the church is in you. It's all about your relationship with God and getting to know Him personally. It's not about your glistening steeples, your mega churches, your big bank account, your title or position, or your emeritus title, but it's about true intimacy with the Father Himself.

God has brought the church to the altar itself, It's time for the deception, and the chameleon spirit to end. Ask yourself as a leader in ministry can you preach when the pews are empty? Can you preach when the tithes and offerings are not so plentiful, can you preach to the man and woman on the streets where the true ministry is, and if so will you be truthful in your hearts to take care of those lambs for God? God's Legacy, what story will you be able to tell?

We are living in the "New Age" Church which will not acknowledge, and believe things without one living what they preach. It's important to find your true identity and not allow anyone to deceive you about who you are. Prayer is the key to escape deception. Allow God to heal your hurt and your wounds. Love God with your whole heart, and look to Him for direction.

Nevertheless, there are some very good leaders in ministry. However, be watchful and aware of the deception that lingers such as: Those who say they are glad for you but are jealous of who you are: those who say they are your friend and they got your back, but they really don't: and those who say I love you, but it's a love-hate relationship. Use wisdom and clear discernment in all your dealings and ask God for understanding to overcome and escape the pitfalls of deception. Ask Him to bring people into your life that will have your back and help you grow. Indeed, the chameleon spirit is real, and that spirit is being exposed. Stand and be like Joshua; knowing that God still fights our battles or be like Elizabeth; knowing that God is almighty and the giver of life.

When it comes to remembering the church, the power, and the Legacy of God one old time hymn comes to mind," Tell Me The Story of Jesus, I Love To Hear". If indeed you are displaying the chameleon deceptive spirit one may ask, after all of your manipulation and deception, "What kind of story will they tell of you and in the end what legacy will you leave? One thing for certain no matter what you have done or been through God still loves you and wants the best for your life. Therefore, give your life to Him. Let Him lead and guide you and rewrite your story so you can have a great legacy to tell. The Bible says, *"A wholesome tongue is a tree of life: but perverseness therein is a breach in the spirit." (Proverbs 15:4) With God you **"WIN."***

CHAPTER 3

STEERING:
SUBMISSION & AUTHORITY

CHAPTER 3

STEERING:
SUBMISSION & AUTHORITY

What domineering factor is holding on and affecting your thoughts?

Is it to give away your soul, or do you give away your peace?

"Do nothing from selfish ambition or conceit, but in humility count others more significant than yourselves." (KJV, Philippians 2:3) Steering is something that parents do with their children to help guide and discipline them. Therefore, some forms of control is good yet when taken out of context and used for one's own selfish good it can be deadly and misleading. Indeed there should be guidelines and rules in the church, but when it is extended into a form of control and mind games it becomes a deadly act. Some leaders use control on their members which engulfs their daily lives, finances, family and friends.

There are leaders who want to control every move of their congregation their interactions, bank accounts, and conversations which can turn into abuse and manipulation. They ask the members to give thousands of dollars to get a word of prophecy at their services, and at times take more than one offering. It appears the members are paying to receive a word from God that is given to them so freely or they are paying for a healing.

Some leaders who are controlling can make a plea to the congregation and make them feel guilty for not following the rules of engagement. Examples of the pleas include: everyone has to dressed a specific way to enter the church, or give a certain amount to be blessed. Some leaders say it is inappropriate to wear makeup, pants, play sports, take birth control, etcetera, yet they are not the "perfect saint". There are other leaders who talk about members in the congregation from the pulpit to shame them or to bring them into compliance. Others try to degrade them for not paying their tithes, or giving a certain amount during an anniversary service per member of the household. This can occur without anyone asking or caring if that household can pay their bills, have food to eat, or if they are on the verge of being put out. Yet, they continue to plea for the last dime they have in their pocket, making them feel guilty for not giving. They attack their lack of faith, and their character while they go home in their nice vehicles, to their beautiful homes. Howbeit, that they should teach the members how to fish so they can be able to take care of themselves better, and be able to give and help the church and their community.

At time leaders may show their authority by slighting certain ministers in their ministry by ignoring them, not inviting them to functions, telling them when they can fellowship and with whom. They tell them what shoes and clothing they can wear to their ministerial schools, how they can wear their hair, and what they can eat not caring or realizing they may not have the funds to maintain those standards imposed upon them. The controller is mainly concerned with "Do as I say or else" which is their motto, otherwise you are disobedient.

An example is a couple whose home was going into foreclosure and they had to come up with the money to keep the bank from taking it. At the time this occurred they had the money but there was a church function and they gave what they had to be a part of the giving. They didn't want to be left out when the call for money was made and the names of the members who gave was mentioned. As a result, in their minds they thought the church would help them out since they gave so willingly and diligently to the church. Howbeit, they ended up losing their home, getting a divorce and leaving the church. They were memorized why they found out the church referred them to social services who had no funds to assist, and it was mentioned to them the church was not a social service organization. One may ask should there have been a social services to assist the members when needed or do the members not count when they are in need of help?

People appear to be mesmerized when it comes to the offerings at times, especially by those who can woo the crowd with how much money they raise. There are also those members who feel they are privileged because of what they give. They march around to the offering bucket and give so everyone can see the largest bill they pull out of their pockets as another form of manipulation.

Correction is to be done by the leader as necessary to help train those in leadership roles so they can know how to deal with those in their congregation. However, when it is done out of malice or to show one's authority it can be a sin, if there is bias within the leader.

Controlling of the mind and submission is a huge practice in some churches where families are manipulated and controlled through mind games by their leader. Women become sex slaves and their children become community property and are sexually abused. Some people live under these conditions for years before they break free. Other churches don't believe in using medication which can bring harm to the individual who is suffering from an illness, yet, they and their families remain as church members. Meanwhile, couples have open sex like an orgy and women are seen as church whores which is alright by the church. They believe in winning souls at any cost even the cost of their bodies. (Smithson & Adamson, 1994)

At times it takes years for these congregates to get the courage and mindset to take their families and leave. Control and manipulation is a "beast" and can be very dangerous.

Some leaders believe in having several spouses, where if one doesn't work out they can get rid of the one they currently have and get another. They have houses where their members can stay that are not kept well, and have the members go out daily to raise funds on the streets. Other leaders have their members apply for food stamps and give it for the group. Being a woman could be treacherous in some of these church groups. Children are not allowed to go to public school and if born into the groups they adapt to the behavior patterns. (Tewa, 2017).

There are also churches that hide babies of girls that were pregnant in their religious sector, or were sold on the market as a donation. Quite a few of these religious communities had contracted diseases and were medically neglected. Over 800 graves for babies were found from girls who had dealt with the nuns in Tuam. (Sixsmith, 2014). Several nuns are speaking out now regarding being raped and having children by clergy. Many of the children they gave birth to were hidden, and the vows of celibacy have been broken by many and not talked about. "Today some of those children have met their actual parents and have built a bond with them despite the shame." (Miller, 2019).

God did not intend for us to have fear of our leaders in the church or to be controlled by them, but to be taught, guided, protected, and loved by them. The Bible says *"For God hath not given us the spirit of fear; but of power, and of love, and of a sound mind."* (KJV, 2 Timothy 1:7).

Forms of control and abuse comes in all denominations worldwide. It doesn't matter about the status quo, economic background, beliefs, upbringing, etc, No matter where you go abuse, control, and manipulation is found in some type of way and needs to be addressed in ministry everywhere. Life is a journey, and there are many twists and turns. God is continuing to uncover things that are hidden in ministry to make them right. Praise His Holy Name. *Ask yourself who and what are you holding onto, and how does it affect your life and peace of mind?* The word of the Lord says - *"My grace is sufficient for you; for My strength is made perfect in weakness." (KJV, 2 Corinthians 12:9).*

The Essence of a Teardrop's Prayer

Sometimes a mere tear drop can bring agonizing pain, and at times travailing prayer can get you through the pain. Yet, each yield's it's own results how ever intense the pain, and each has it's own unique story and history to tell. The story may be joyful, it may be full of life, then at times it may be sorrowful, remorseful, and full of strife. However, be the journey of the tears you may have shed, it may have yielded quick results, or it may have been something you dread. Yet the sower of the tears may be far from being praised, far from life's successes, and far from engulfing pain. When they ask the tear drop what is it that you proclaim, what clear purpose have you gained, and what is it that remains? The tear drop proudly speaks and releases, I have a purpose to help you release a healing even though it may cause pain, and out of that pain comes healing which remains.

I, the tear drop sometimes help remind you that there is hope for you and help you to navigate your life while realizing which way to go. At times I come because of joy, ecstasy, urgency, or a kind and tender touch. For I am a tear drop and you are in need of me to bring hope and refresh you when there seems to be no relief. I can press you forward, or I may set you back at times, it depends on who you follow, coupled with prayer in mind.

I recommend prayer because he is my partner and it's the best way to communicate with God. He has a connection with the one who loves you best, and is near and dear to God's heart. We work together for the Bible says, *" And God will wipe away every tear from their eyes, there shall be no more death, nor sorrow, nor crying. There shall be no more pain for the former things have passed away". (Revelation 21:4 KJV.)* Your tear drop is like prayer that flows freely from the heart which is attended by God through your prayers.

Whereas, God makes everything brand new even after your tears. He so sweetly consoles and molds you in His hands, and so deeply cares for you. Ask yourself who is there after the tears, and the pain, and can they carry your heartache? God is. He has not forgotten you nor left you. Call Him and He is there, cry out to Him and He is there. Pray to Him and He is there, even in the midst of your tears.

Prayer, a tear drops friend which helps to bring you to the place God has for you. A place of joy, peace and comfort. A place where love dwells, the protection and sweetness of God.

God is nudging at your heart, especially during the times when you say, "I just don't believe, or it looks like HE has forgotten me." You need to know from the beginning of time God placed you in His hands, before you were conceived. He talked with you, prayed for you and prepared you to be placed in your mother's womb. Can you imagine God knowing you before you knew yourself? How awesome is that? He positioned you, and clasped you in His hands so that He could breathe the breath of life into the beautiful soul you are now. How fantastic is that, He thought about you before time existed for you to be here. As you were developing God introduced technology through the medical men and women in your time to see how you were progressing. This showed up through what they call an embryo and fetus that needed to be fed and taken care of. So, He placed you inside a warm, soft womb, which we call “Mamma,” and there He and His angels continued to communicate with you until the timing of your birth.

When a sonogram is done the embryo can be seen in the prayer position showing they are still connected to the Father (until birth). “What a wonderful connection!” Once the baby is born, ironically, a disconnection takes place. They are born where a void takes the warm place of the connection yielding a desire to reconnect with God, which only God can fill. Some refer to this as a “Quantum Leap' which is an abrupt transition. We know that His grace is sufficient for us, and therefore, we gain strength in knowing He is there for us. God will grant us grace to rejoice in the most vulnerable times of our lives. He will accept us despite our past, or what we’re going through, For the blood of Christ can cleanse us and make us whole again.

Know that your teardrops are precious no matter what you're going through. Whether it be tears of joy, strength or courage, a prayer can connect one back to the Father again. Make up your own mind, and step out in the waters, lift your hands and say “I’m in”. Be free from sin, be born again, run to Christ, shed your tears, cleanse your soul, and live again. For the essence of a teardrop and a prayer may help cleanse your soul. God can intervene in your life, and you'll find out the true treasure hidden inside..

CHAPTER 4

A CRACK IN THE WALL: SHADY BEHAVIOR

CHAPTER 4

A CRACK IN THE WALL: SHADY BEHAVIOR

Can your heart be mended through a broken crack?

One must ask is it evil to act on strange thoughts, or is it

an acquired behavior?

Ministry is to be a defense for the church to help those who need to come closer to God and to teach them how to live. However, when the defense is down there is either a crack in the wall or a leak in the dam. We are living in the time to be about Kingdom business and not to elude the temptations and boastful things man produces in the church. Competing with who's who, if I can make the right connections what will I become, who knows my name, who can help me, and who holds my destiny in their hands has become a trophy of gold. We are in the era where man must make a decision whether to be obedient to God, or to be rebellious and follow the pathway that has been presented to them. For when this happens there is a crack in the wall.

A person cannot live in the past, with the wounds, hurts and mockery that binds them or stops them from moving forward. Where do you stand when they say they hold your destiny in their hands and try to diminish your hopes and dreams? They lock you up and throw away the key and say you'll never be free again? By the way, don't forget you owe them.

Where do you stand my friend when God is calling you to a greater work, yet the fear inside of you overwhelms the assignment of your heart? Tell me where do you stand when they try to snatch the very anointing God has placed in your hands, and say you're not worth very much? Where do you stand when you know God has called you and men ask what's wrong with you, or why are you doing that crazy thing? It seems there's a crack in the wall of ministry that is full of contention. It appears if someone does something different and the powers that be have not given them the go ahead or permission then it is not the right path to go down. Why do you ask: because you are leading the people astray and it's of the devil-how sad that the leaders fight change in growth. This kind of behavior divides the church.

There should be an appreciation of the old and the new together because God is doing a new thing but He has not forgotten the old.

In fact, He models and reminds us of the old so that we can appreciate where we have come from and where He is taking us. Sounds confusing, well now is the time to get your mind on track because the time is coming even in America where you will have to decide whom you will serve. The time will come where you must decide whether you will stand for the ways of man or stand for the ways of God. I urge you not to be caught up in the spiritual wilderness and to be prepared for the surroundings and changes coming to our world. I also urge you to get closer to God and if you have left Him rekindle your relationship with Him again.

The Lord is making a call to the United States of America to come back to Him. Go back to your roots, renew your mind and faith. Fear the Lord and honor Him. Repent, and pull down the religious thoughts in your mind that no one is right but you and yours. God has many soldiers you know not of. They may not look like you, act like you, walk, or dress like you, but they are the image of the Father and have His DNA.

As time goes on even on the soil of the United States we may experience war and blood shed from other nations. Therefore, prepare your family to believe in God and learn to pray. I urge you to seal up the cracks in your life, your ministry, your heart and love one another! Learn to work with each other, for your religion and faith is not greater than the next man. The backbiting done in the church must end because it grieves the heart of God. Stop esteeming yourself more highly than you ought and humble yourself before the "Almighty God." Ask yourself, will you sell your brother or sister out, or will you stand for the righteousness of God? Is there a crack in your wall, and if so how will you fill it up?

A person with a broken spirit needs your encouragement, not your criticism, or your gossiping and mocking spirit. They need a loving heart to accept who they are, and help embrace the miracle God can do in their lives. The chains and bonds of depression, anxiety, discomfort, disappointment, hurt and humiliation can be overcome faster and easier with the help of each other because a hand up is better than a hand down. Lack of understanding, manipulation, control, and fear are chains and bonds that can hold one back.

The Effects Of Gossip In The Church

Pastor Dave Ramsey has a no gossiping policy in his church which states gossiping is "discussing anything negative with someone who can't help solve the problem". In his organization employees are not allowed to gossip and if found out or reported they are fired. Pastor Ramsey believes if employees have a concern they should go straight to the leader and report it. Perhaps this policy appears to help keep down conflict misunderstandings, and lies among congregants, and avoid cracks in the foundation of the church.

Gossiping according to Webster's New World Dictionary is defined as: A person who chatters or repeats idle talk and rumors, esp. about the private affairs of others. (2023, Love To Know).Hearsay and gossip in the church can be very harmful and detrimental to a person's character especially if it is untruth.

Hanging in cliques and gossip groups can be embarrassing in the church and cause friction among members, especially clergy. Some people believe the tongue has armed itself too much. It can cause misunderstandings, break up homes, friendship, and relationships in the church. Some Christians who use these tactics make the victim work at recovering biblical understanding in their environment. It is called "Hearsay vs. Healthy" criticism. (2021, Shellnutt).

As a group of people, we need to mend the crack in the wall and the dam before it breaks and falls. God wants to heal you, give you a breakthrough to go higher, and take someone with you.

We were created to praise God. Go ahead mend that crack in the wall, shake yourself off, and lift your voice of victory to the heavens because you are "Free". Allow God to renew your spirit and reignite fire in your bones. Let Him in; all He needs is a crack that needs mending, and He can fill it for a lifetime with new wine. Take a quantum leap into the supernatural power of God! Become more intimate with Him, and allow his love to fill the crack in you which will take you to an epic euphoria with Him that spills over to others through you.

Ask God to change your DNA, your mind and your will. Consider how you're building your church and ministry. Hold your head up and walk in power, grace, joy, integrity, confidence and love. *"For which of you, intending to build a tower, sitter not down first, and counteth the cost. Whether he have sufficient to finish it?"* (Luke 14:28, KJV) Perhaps a tear drop may fall, or a travailing prayer may be prayed, yet in the midst of it all, God is there. I urge you to rise up, be healed, mend the crack in you, mend the crack in ministry, so you can mend the crack in broken lives that need to be healed. Mature in Christ and help others grow by grace, and excellence.

CHAPTER 5

THE COPY WRITTEN WORD OF GOD

CHAPTER 5

THE COPY WRITTEN WORD OF GOD

Is there enough money in the world for you to pay the debt you owe?

"For we are unto God a sweet savour of Christ, in them that are saved, and in them that perish: To the one we are the savour of death unto death; and to the other the savour of life unto life. And who is sufficient for these things? For we are not as many, which corrupt the word of God: but as of sincerity, but as of God, in the sight of God speak we in Christ." (2 Corinthians 2:15-17, KJV).

The exclusive legal way to publish, reproduce a book, music, or literary in this disposition is through a copyright. We have the Bible which is believed by many that God inspired scholarly men to write who knew how to put the words together to scribe the Bible so we could read it and comprehend what He wanted us to know. It is from this collaboration that it appears Christ is the motivator, mediator, and a go between for the written word of God.

It also appears the Holy Spirit is the executor, producer, and publisher of the word of God which comes to teach us, and this somehow makes them all sole proprietors of the "Word of God" which is known to man as the – The Bible.

From the beginning of time the word was God and the word still belongs to God. God gave man the word as a way of communication to let them know who He is, to teach them His ways, and inform them how to live. Even today the scriptures is still a word for all times, a word that is used in and out of season all over the world. The disciples who became Apostles were not commissioned to go out and charge the people for the word, healing or casting out demons, but were instructed "freely you have received, freely give."

Christ did not tell the blind man "I can't heal you until you bring me alms or an offering". Jesus didn't tell the woman with an issue of blood who touched the hem of His garment and the virtue went out of Him. He didn't negotiate with her to give him $5,000 and she would be healed or get a word of prophecy, yet he freely healed her. He didn't charge a wager for people to come hear him preach, but he allowed them to come freely and receive the word from His Father.

Some Psychiatrists believe all genuine ministries in the Lord cannot have an advanced price tag before the ministry is given because it is no longer ministry, but commerce, employ, trade and entertainment. Christ gave all that He had to help the church and the world: shouldn't we give all that we have and do the same?

I do understand that finances are definitely needed in the church in order for it to stay afloat and be ran. However, at what cost do we exploit the people to engage in the business of money? What gives ministers justification too sell and make bank on the word of God that is given to them so freely?

The dreaded money line, paying for a prophetic word, a mite for a prayer cloth, or anointed oil, and how much does the word cost? How much is God charging you to have permission to preach His word, sell tapes of His word, sell videos of His word, make fliers and posters of His scripted word that you didn't even write? Many ministers utilize thrombolytics which is a system that breaks down blood clots to help the patient live and prevent strokes. Some ministers have a team of professionals that preach to the people and focus on breaking down the word of God to help them save themselves from death and sin at a cost for their deliverance. Yet out of all of this how much do they pay to use the word of God when it is so freely given for their usage?

Paying For A Prophecy: Is It Abuse?

Many people discredit prophets and the word of knowledge they give due to false prophecies and misuse of some clergy wanting people to pay for a word or wanting them to give a huge amount of money to get a prophecy. Therefore, some people don't believe in prophets, and mock them. Others abuse the prophets who are legit and real that truly hear from God.

As the church continues they will need a prophet to help them along the way. However, there are some people today that abuse their office as a prophet and expect people to give large sums of money to receive a prophetic word. One bishop for certain asks people to give large sums of money then they give them a word.

After giving that large sum of money and receiving the word the person is contacted again to give another large sum of money and are told they need to sew a seed to receive another word. This can become a form of abuse, and it makes one wonder what happens to the people who cannot pay the large sum of money? Do they just not get a word, or does God not have anything to say to them?

I have experienced this type of treatment and it does not feel good. It definitely makes you wonder what is the catch? Is this for their own financial gain, or is the Lord pleased with a person paying for a word? Corruption is running rampant in the church and some people who leave the church due to corrupted leadership. Some clergy inform the congregation this is a sacrificial offering and after you give a substantial amount you will receive a word. This puts some congregants on edge while others desperately want a word from the Lord, so they give. One wonders about this successful leadership, and people ask "who should we hold responsible? " (2021, Allen).

Just think how much is God charging you for permission to preach His word, sell tapes of His word, for videos, to make fliers and posters of His scripted word that you didn't even write? Many ministers utilize thrombolytics which is a system that breaks down blood clots to help the patient live and prevent strokes. Some ministers have a team of professionals that preach to the people that focus on breaking down the word of God to help them save themselves from death and sin at a cost for their deliverance. Yet out of all of this how much do they pay to use the word of God when it is so freely given for their usage?

Then there are those who have battles and compete with each other in the word and believe the understanding of the word in the Bible only belongs to them. Some ministers believe the word should only be spoken by men and not women, others believe the word is to be spoken by all, and there are some who compare themselves and try to outdo their peers. Grace and gifts are given to all, and no one is to dominate or judge the other, but work together. Ephesians 4:7 says "*But unto every one of us is given grace according to the measure of the gift of Christ." (KJV).*

*What is in your hands, can they see the real you, an*d has money made you? In order to know what is in your hands one must first understand and know what they have. God is asking do you really know who I am, do you really know what is in your hands, and what I have given to you? Do you really realize that all power is in His hands, and that He can fix your problems with the blink of an eye, yet every thing could be taken from you overnight? Who do you say that I am when you push me to the side, and get engulfed in your fame on my word? God is looking at the inner thoughts of man and their very soul. The word of God was not given for men to argue and debate about, but it is to be used as a reference for life.

God is urging you to truly get to know Him, and not just His word. We have the awesome love of a divine Savior in our hands: We are part of the rich heritage of Abraham, David, Enoch, the Alpha and Omega, The Beginning and The End. Our heritage is from the one who can make you whole, cleanse you from your sins, be a powerful weapon when you need one; not just a word. God is saying, "Do you know what is in your hands?" Can you see the real Me for I am way beyond what your mind can imagine. I AM more than just a Word?

I wonder if God rolled back the heavens and shouted with a loud voice through the clouds "Pay Up" would those who utilize His word be able to pay the price for the time and messages they have gotten from the word? My dear one how much would you owe? Would you be able to pay for the breath of life given to you?

Would you be able to pay for the intellect handed down to you? Would you be able to pay for the wisdom and knowledge you gained through the word of God that you never paid a dime for but dare to charge His people to obtain a prophecy? If you had an order to Pay Up today, would you have enough assets to pay, could you afford the ability to stay in His word at all cost?

The anointing that God showered on you through His word, ask yourself how much would that cost? Would your bill be too high, or would you still have a place to live? Freely you received, yet you don't freely give. How much would your life be worth without the copy written word of God?

Some ministers have made it into a business, but who gave them permission? They are captivated by the allure of the marketplace, the driven ministry, the idea of money changing hands, and the fame it may bring. God is merciful and allows each one of us to preach His word to save the souls of men. An old song says, "What Shall I Render Unto God, What Shall I Give"? His Word is priceless.

Truly the laborer is worthy of his hire, but at what price does it become a stench in the nostrils of God? Being in ministry is not an easy cross to bear. Mother Teresa mentioned, "The founder of a religious order has to carry the cross acutely, for they have a lot to suffer." Indeed there is power in those who carry the word and much influence. Yet one may carry the influence of hatred, or the influence of favor, but one must bring the word. Believe me there is no free ride in ministry or in life, but true ethics should be practiced in everything we do for Christ.

The copy written word of God, asks yourself who really owns it, what is the cost to carry it, and what must I do to continue to utilize it? Psalms 119 says *"Thy word have I hid in my heart that I might not sin against thee."* (KJV). We must remember God for everything belongs to Him. Remember the sweet aroma and fragrance of His word. Ponder on what type of fragrance are you leaving, for you received the word of God freely, shall you not do the same to freely give to others?

CHAPTER 6

HOPE - SAFEGUARD THE LAMB

CHAPTER 6

HOPE - SAFEGUARD THE LAMB

"What would you give in exchange for your soul?"
Matthew 8:17

Help me, help me is the cry of the soul in this dispensation of time. Some say good leadership should protect, pray for, teach and empower the lambs and sheep they watch over. Others believe they are to control, guide them according to their rules and regulations and make sure they are accountable for their actions. One could ask should the ministry leaders bring peace or compliance to their congregation? Are they zealous for their own needs, or the needs of the people?

Oh how precious a jewel is the soul of man. We must protect, preserve, and nurture it. Our soul is the inner part of our being and without it we are lost, empty, barren and incomplete. Our soul is a vital divine part of our humanness, a corporate divine entity which is called a spirit that survives after death. It is a central part of every man's being, a perfect embodiment of an intangible quality that we all seem to possess which engulfs our nature, emotions, and our righteousness. The soul touches our perceptions and sensations that relates to our intuition. It is susceptible to our responses of life, our awareness and our emotions. The soul was created in God's divine glory and is so complex man cannot quite understand it, but knows that it exist. The soul I speak of cries out for "redress" to make things right, and for us to amend our ways. The soul is weeping and utters a call of grievance, a call of repentance.

The very soul of man makes an urgent appeal and proclaims righteous living with heartfelt tears. It demands an awareness of destruction down the road, it suggests a remedy, and gives a solution at the same time. This soul of man that God created, this inanimate matter, this spirit that He placed within a temporary temple called man to breathe is calling out "help me, help me to live." The soul of man is ignored many times over, and sometimes even sold. This wonderful spirit from God which influences our lives, cares for our well being, and guides us to a better life. It longs for and desires to live again, to be protected and safeguarded from sin. This rejuvenated quality within our souls possess responses to stimuli and directs us back to God to help fill the void within our inner man…

From birth the soul is attached to God. This may be seen vicariously through a baby in the womb where they are in the fetal position and it appears they are praying. One could only wonder are they truly connected still to God? This sweet spirit within you from birth responds to the call of the Master no matter who you are. One may ask "what would you give in exchange for your soul? Would you rather have money, jewelry, fame, fortune, your name in lights, or riches untold? (Mark 8:36) says, *"For what shall profit a man, if he shall gain the whole world and lose his own soul?"* Prosperity is a part of the kingdom but wisdom should be used in all things big and small.

The favor of God is an awesome thing to have on one's life. Some may ask how do they get the favor of God because as a servant of God it helps and encourages the soul. The Bible says, *"For thou, Lord, wilt bless the righteous; with favour wilt thou compass him as with a shield." (Psalm 5:12, KJV.)* Having favor from the Lord is a shield in our lives. It could be stated that this is exceptional favor of kindness, and liking from the Lord where He shows His grace upon a person. This gives "Hope" and the courage to stand and go the distance knowing that God is present. It also takes away fear and doubt to build trust in God knowing that He will lead them on.

When getting to really know the Lord a person may hear the sound of the wind, but it may be a different sound than what is heard by others. Precaution should be used in sharing about this sound which comes from the Lord, especially within dreams. This safeguards your thoughts which God has placed in you until they are cultivated to fruition. Prematurely some have had their dreams put down or blocked because they were so excited and told the wrong person which blocked access to their purpose at that time. Learning from the experience of Joseph being so excited about his dream yet his brothers became jealous and tried to stop his progress by throwing him into a pit. (But God) ---- prevailed and made his life a living testimony that has gone on and on for years as an example of the favor of the Lord upon his life, and grace.

Therefore, there is definitely hope for the lamb. Be mindful that when you put your faith and trust in God things and people from your past will try to interfere, but they will know that God is in control of your destiny which will have impact to others around the world. Remind yourself of who you are and whose you are. Cut off the rift raft, shake the dust off your feet and move forward. God will blow your mind, just say "Yes" to His will and run like the wind. Is there hope for the lamb? Most definitely!

Some say men and women can't work together unless the woman totally submits to the man and meets his sexual needs which they believe is submission. I would say God says for both man and woman to submit to each other, and for them both to build and dominate together, not challenging or being in competition with each other...The woman is more than a sex toy. Some leaders say "She should stay in her place." That is true and "her place is In God." There is nothing like a man and woman working together to fulfill the purpose on their lives and to reach their destiny God has planned for them together God has given us all a brain (for creativity) through thought, and we should allow each other to use "that brain" for His good will, and to help others.

It has been proven that there is nothing more powerful than a couple working together for God and impacting people around the world while carrying out the will of God side by side. This includes supporting and lifting each other up. Myles Munroe stated, "When purpose is not known, abuse is inevitable." We should learn the true purpose God has for all mankind on earth. Abuse can be avoided and overcome by caring, respecting, loving each other, and realizing we each have something to offer, whether male or female. It is a beautiful thing, not to have a dominating system which can bring joy and favor in our lives.

I urge you to develop healthy boundaries, and lift up your head, because you deserve more. Surrender your life to the one who can truly fulfill you, and touch the heart of God. I pray that the spirit of abuse is broken over your lives, your ministry, family, emotions, and your mind! God loves you so very much. Be sensitive to the Holy Spirit, and God will lead you in the right direction. He will impart meaning to your lives, wisdom, knowledge, and leadership skills on how you can reach His little lambs, and bring them to Christ. Shalom

Beware My Aching Heart For I Am Just A Lamb

(The Lamb's Virtual Poetic Experience)

I am my brother's keeper that is the golden rule: yet they sit beside me in church and it's cold, even chilled. It is colder than the snow outside, chillier than an ice cube, yet I greet and speak for I am my brother's keeper, *and* they turn me away. They have their cliches and groups. They even dress alike showing elitism can't you see. Hmm, I wonder dear heart should I wear blue on a Monday, black on a Sunday and will that bring me closer to my Savior? My heart is pure, so soft on the inside. I can hear God calling me, and shaping me in His glory. Should my heart be aching for where my Father does not dwell? Should my heart that is pure be broken because they don't know Him that well? Father, what should I do, for my heart is being *subjected* to control, manipulation, and scorn. I am left all alone, but Lord this is (Church)

Their positions are beautiful, but do they say who they really are? O' dear heart be careful, be careful of what you see, for some of these folks will surely harm the lamb in thee. For I'm sitting in the sanctuary but no one seems to see me. They can't see the pain I'm in or the love that I seek? Can anyone see my *brokenness*, or perhaps I'm in the wrong *place*? Thank you God, that I have you to help me, because my heart is put of place.

I want to know my friend, would God be welcomed in *your* church if He came? Can you take care of the lamb, and is Jesus manifested in you, or would you ignore the lamb because it's all about you? I pray you make a change and welcome the God of heaven and earth into your hearts for who am I to say I was ignored, for I am just a lamb.

CHAPTER 7

A DOUBLE-MINDED MAN

CHAPTER 7

A DOUBLE-MINDED MAN

Could you follow a leader with indecisive and wavering behavior, or would you be profitable and healthy from affluent encouragement?

Which path shall I go, which path shall I choose? Shall I run like the wind or stay until the end? Are the doctrines quite right or should I take a flight? It doesn't make sense, and I'm confused most of the time. Hmm, I wonder could this *really* be God? Are you in a congregation and have asked yourself these questions? Does the doctrine, beliefs, and ways of doing things have you questioning what is right? Have you been told to denounce what you believe and take on a whole new segment and way of doing things?

Indeed, one should study the word for themselves, and search the scriptures to find out and get a revelation of what *is* right. Trying to go by your own thoughts could shift one into a stormy world of chaos. Just think, does your spirit have peace, or are you just following the crowd? Is there a check in your spirit about what the heck you should do now, I urge you my friend to take it to the Lord in prayer, because confusion is definitely not the way of the Lord.

The Bible speaks of a double-minded man and says, *"A double-minded man is unstable in all his ways." (James 1:8, KJV).* This means if a man has dual thoughts in his mind where he is divided in his thinking perhaps another may be apprehensive to follow him. An example of this is if they are divided in seeing one doctrine over another, yet they are not certain which one to believe, which may leave the members in a confused state. The Greek word " dipsychos" means uncertain, doubting, and divided interest. Questions to ponder when it comes to (belief) is why am I thinking this way, and what is causing my mind to waver?

Do you really know who you are, and do you have one set of rules for one group, and another set for the other? (Shirlaw-Ferreir, 2022). Other questions to think on include do what I believe really meet my needs or am I hungry for something more and can't seem to find it? You may ask yourself do you get the real revelation of what the void is that needs to be filled, and if not why not?

Deborah JohnsnDeborah JohnsnWhat is "holding you captive" to be divided in your mind and thoughts? At times we may feel we need and want to get closer to God but don't know how. We may find ourselves set in our own ways of doing things, and making up our own set of rules to accomplish this. Perhaps we take on the task of trying to approach God and His deity in a different way because inside we feel we need more and have a longing that just is not satisfied.

However, from the leaders directive those thoughts and reasoning may be forced on others if we are not careful. This may cause one to lead others astray. Maybe, just maybe you might find yourself in a situation that could throw you off track. Perhaps this could come from listening to someone regarding a doctrine you may not understand, or a thought you are not clear on that can carry over to the people under your ministry. This could cause division, and problems for those who don't agree with the new mindset.

In your life as a leader you need to address the challenges that come along with change and adjust so it can help you mature and grow. Having a spiritual leader to confide in also helps one to get re-grounded as well, and helps you to be aligned within the will of God, without becoming a manipulator, a controller, or feeling you are always the victim.

At times a leader can believe they are so right without really consulting God and are ready to put a person out because they don't believe in what they believe is the truth. Therefore, one must be careful of telling someone "We have to find out where you fit in…" We must understand and ask, what did God think about when He chose you? Did He say oops, first I have to find out who you are, where you fit in, and what you think? Hmm. God looked at you, changed your heart and mind and took you in despite all of your fears, anxieties, lack of knowledge, and insecurities. *He found a unique spot for you in His heart.*.The Bible states, *"Draw near to God and He will draw near to you. Cleanse your hands, you sinners; and purify your hearts, you "double-minded." (James 4:8).*

Doubting who you are and why you are called to ministry can be a problem in your everyday life. Not trusting yourself can also carry over into you not trusting anyone, and not being able to work with others. Micromanaging everything and everyone may be a sign of needing help. Counseling is always a good thing to help manage the thoughts that divide and waver in our minds. Seek out assistance when needed. Yes, prayer is the key, but at times a mental health professional can be very beneficial.

God is faithful and He loves us so dearly that He places helpers in our lives to get us through certain situations and rough times when we can't navigate through those waters by ourselves. When we align ourselves, our minds and our thoughts with God, He directs our paths as we step out to lead others to Christ it enriches our lives as well.

Red Flags That May Lead To Abuse In Ministry

(2021, Annon & Aten)

Hero Worship Goal Confusion

Lack of Accountability

"Protection" of the Institution

In your life as a leader you need to address the challenges that come along with change and adjust so it can help you mature and grow. Having a spiritual leader to confide in also helps one to get re-grounded as well, and helps you to be aligned within the will of God, without becoming a manipulator, a controller, or feeling you are always the victim.

Some Signs of Toxic Leaders

(2023, Kocka).

- Divide people behind the scenes
- Believe loyalty only goes one way
- Display spiritual elitism and a superiority
- Mistake their manipulations for "change."

Suppress dissent and critical thinking.

Make decisions behind closed doors.

Have an excessive focus on finances

Divide people behind the scenes

Lack of transparency in decisions

Suppress dissent and critical thinking.

Make decisions behind closed doors.

Disregard the emotional well-being

Attack the values of others publicly

Misuse scripture to justify behaviors.

Discriminate against certain groups

Make slights, insults, and even threats

Display exclusionary practices and cliques

Encourage blind loyalty and submission.

Structure leadership so they are unaccountable

Regularly remind others that they are in charge.

Make degrading comments on appearances

Send others to do their "dirty" work

Signs of Successful Leadership
(2023, Ministry Answers)

Successful ministry leaders have a deep understanding of their congregation's needs and are able to communicate those needs effectively to their team and congregation. They also need:

- Charisma
- Communication
- Organization
- Humility Passion
- Strong Moral Values Good
- Strong Work Ethics
- Able To Handle Stress & Long Hours
- Conflict Resolution Empathy
- Forgiving
- Sense of Timing

Doubting who you are and why you are called to ministry can be a problem in your everyday life. Not trusting yourself can also carry over into you not trusting anyone, and not being able to work with others. Micromanaging everything and everyone may be a sign of needing help. Counseling is always a good thing to help manage the thoughts that divide and waver in our minds. Seek out assistance when needed. Yes, prayer is the key, but at times a mental health professional can be very beneficial.

God is faithful and He loves us so dearly that He places helpers in our lives to get us through certain situations and rough times when we can't navigate through those waters by ourselves. When we align ourselves, our minds and our thoughts with God, He directs our paths as we step out to lead others to Christ and it enriches our lives as well.

I Give Him Praise

My heart deeply yearns for the formal expression to say, "Good morning, King Jesus – let's have a great day". He's so worthy and desirable that words cannot be said. He puts a song in my heart so I can face another day. He's more than just a value, or a measure of equation, for He has the natural ability to help me, develop me, and send me on my way. My Lord, my King always knows just what to say. When you feel that your mind may waver, and your thoughts get disarrayed. Come back to God and allow Him to renew your mind, and your thoughts. "Draw near to Him" yes He knows your heart, and the things you need to do. Don't run away from God, but allow Him to refresh you. Praise Him for the revelation and the newness within you. He says be attentive my child and not authoritative where you are so offended that you can't accept the help I have sent you. Try to communicate and build a relationship with those you work with instead of trying to find things to criticize them for. Always looking for the bad in someone and alerting others to watch out for them without getting to know them poses a problem for you as a good leader. Remember God always sees and understands.

Blessings

CHAPTER 8

DON'T TAKE THE GLORY:

A EAGLE'S STORY

CHAPTER 8

DON'T TAKE THE GLORY:

A EAGLE'S STORY

I grew up in the C.O.G.I.C. (Church of God In Christ) Faith as a child, and later became a part of the SDA (Seventh Day Adventist) Faith. From both of these religious groups I developed a good firm foundation in ministry, learned more about better eating habits, faith, and leaning on the Lord. I learned to operate in the church in every office and have developed a sense of intimacy with God. As my life went through its ups and downs, I learned God is my refuge and strength no matter what I face or go through.

At times I wondered if God was with me, but He somehow would always let me know He was there, and how beautiful He really is. I've seen Him do miracles, and the impossible over and over again. I experienced times when people took me for granted, and thought I wasn't much of anything because they were higher up, and I suppose somehow they were the perfect man according to their own tactics and perception.

If you were not on their level they did not have time for you, and would let you know you didn't qualify to be with them, to be in an position, or hang out with them even though you were a highly anointed minister. It's like they would only recognize you when the elites were not around. I believe they forgot about the trials one had to go through to obtain the true anointing of God. Nevertheless, it doesn't matter how they tried to break you, they couldn't break what God was holding together in you.

They didn't realize God had you in His loving arms, and was taking you through a trial and test that only He could bring you out of, not their discipline, harsh remarks, or offenses.

It must be realized that when God gets through with a person their mind, thoughts, heart, and soul become brand new. They may not fit in where you want them to, but God will raise them out of the ashes of their past, and they will rise up on wings like an Eagle to become that precious, beautiful minister and leader He has ordained them to be. Remember, God makes everything extraordinary, and breath-taking new, to where no one can touch it. When God gets in your life, and rewrites *your story*, who can come up against what He says? NO ONE!!

When man thinks He has you at your lowest and weakest point, and is determined not to let you go up and shuts all doors, so you can't go any further to stop you, God steps in and creates a new image of who you are and presents you to the world. When they are determined to force you to submit to their tactics, doctrine, and ways, God steps up, and says "not so" because I am making them, I am molding them, and reshaping their mind where you won't even recognize them when I'm done.

Be careful leaders who you put down, through your words, actions, cliches, groups, and behavior. God is watching you. As the old folks used to say, "God is looking, and booking." What is God documenting about you and your actions towards the vessels He has chosen? Oh, but I forgot, you are the perfect man or woman of God.

Perhaps there's something wrong inside of a person who gets offended over so many things and always wants one to apologize to them because they are so very hurt, and feel they are constantly disrespected when someone voices an opinion. Perhaps, just maybe that leader should take a look at themselves and their own imperfect life. The Bible says, *"He that is without sin among you. Let him cast the first stone." (John 8:7, KJV)* What is on the inside of the person that is offended so easily, and is so sensitive to every error? What are they really dealing with and what is the real root of the problem inside?

The accusers always want to discipline, but, they are hurt when someone brings a wrong to their attention about themselves. They forgot so easily that every branch on the vine is needed, and they are not the only one with feelings. One should never take pride in who they are or what they have gone through, but always be mindful of the fact it was God that saved them, not themselves.

Sometimes a leader forgets about what happens to the child of God who they constantly put their thumb on their neck. Yet, because they have authority which they feel must be displayed to all not realizing what would happen if God just put a tip of His finger on their neck to display His authority to others about them. A person could ask how much pressure they would feel, and could they handled the pressure and weight of the Lord on them? one could ask who do they really answer to, and is their mentor a true person that hears from God?

What happens when God takes *revenge* on those who have treated His *anointed* wrong? What happens when God says enough, and sends His angels to fight for them? Will the abuser be able to handle the wrath of God, will they run to hide, will there be anywhere to run, or will they fall on their knees and repent?

I urge you to hold on my friend because God will vindicate you, and give you a chance that man could never give. He will raise you up to levels that man cannot bring you to and open doors no one can shut. What happens when God takes revenge? ***Answer***: *Everything changes*, and everything is returned to you full force.

It's not over yet, and as my awesome Pastor Bishop Vernon Richardson said, "You latter days will be greater than your past." Expect to bloom in the midst of the weeds and stand tall in the rain with your head up to the sun. May your blossoms bloom with exuberance so that people will look at you in awe of what the Lord has done! For your greatness is at hand, and no man can stop it. Praise God, stand tall and bloom in the hands of the Lord.

Intimacy and Spiritual Encounters

When I was a child I loved to draw pictures, and I had an experience in my bedroom as I was drawing. I looked up at the ceiling of my room and it opened up where I could see the clouds. I saw beautiful angels all dressed in white ascending and descending on an awesome white ladder, and I just sat there in awe just watching. As I grew older and learned more about God, I got my own apartment. At times, I would come home and unlock the door and start speaking in tongues because the presence of the Holy Ghost met me there.

I traveled quite a bit for work and one day I came home from the airport and was so tired. I sat at the living room table and put my head down. I dreamed angels came and took me to heaven, and I ran across the heavens with them. These angels were children. At that time I was afraid of them, and they let me know it wasn't time yet because I was afraid. I then felt my spirit come back into my body.

As time went on, while I was in my bedroom sitting on my bed I heard this beautiful angelic choir singing. I looked outside but didn't see anyone there, and it got louder. I heard it all throughout my apartment, it was so beautiful. I laid down to sleep and found myself hoovering in the air looking out over the city, watching people move around, and I began to pray for the people. During this time I learned to pray more and became a prayer warrior.

When I moved to New York and began to learn more about the prophetic, I began to see faces of demons, and my discernment became very strong. I started to learn what my gifts were and how to use them. I would smell the lilac of angels and knew when they were around. At times I would feel the angels walking with me, and around me. I went to church and the Pastor told me she saw two angels with me, one on my left and one on my right. Somehow, I knew they were there. I didn't quite understand what was happening to me when I first experienced these things, but I began to realize what I was going on and the fear left. I then moved to Washington State, I learned even more about my gifts and how to use them, and became more intimate with God. I would go to church and the Pastor would call people up for prayer, and would tell me they saw Jesus standing beside me during the service. I then went overseas to South Africa and as I was preaching one of the minister's took a picture and in the picture there was an angel standing beside me in the pulpit as I preached.

I went to Uganda and went to visit a friend's church that had come to the USA. He introduced me and gave me the microphone. As he handed it to me the anointing and fire of God was so strong I ran over the stage prophesying and shaking. At our revival it was like the people were so hungry for God and He was there to feed them. It was like if I could pick up the anointing I would take it bring it back to the USA in my pocket.

A lady came to me after service after I preached in Kenya and wanted prayer. She stated she couldn't have a child and was going to be put out of the village. We prayed and a year later she sent me a picture of her son that she gave birth to. God is so good, all glory and honor goes to Him. I went to dinner with my friends when I returned to the states and they took a picture. In the picture there was a figure of Jesus standing beside me. While I was doing an internship as a Chaplain at a hospital in Puyallup it was like I was baptized by fire that night. I had one death after the other, and was thinking this definitely wasn't for me.

I had never seen so many people die in one day. I then went on break and sat down in the back of the chapel and put my head in my hands. I raised my head up and opened my eyes and saw a cherub that came and took my hand and walked with me. We went to the front of the chapel and there were little baby lions jumping around this huge beautiful golden Lion that had such a gorgeous peaceful light shining like the sun with a glow around it. As I looked at it my spirit calmed down, and I felt such a peace like everything was going to be alright. It was so bright and beautiful until the light permeated the entire chapel. It brought calmness and peace all around the room. It's like Jesus came just to calm my fears. After this *I knew* I would be alright.

Another encounter occurred when my mother became ill and I went home to take care of her before she passed away. She was bedridden and while I was attending to her she rose up and sat up in the bed and stared looking up to the sky while extending her arms towards Christ and the angels coming to get her. I prayed and said "not yet" because I wasn't ready for her to go. I went to church later that week and my Bishop was in town running a revival. He told me that my mother was holding on for me, but she was ready to go. Somehow, that gave me *peace* and by the end of the week, and she went home to be with the Lord. It is *amazing* how God had people there just to help *me* get through those times in my life. Later I went to a revival with another Prophet. On the way home I was riding in the back seat of his car. He kept looking in the mirror *on the way home. A*s he pulled in the driveway, he told me, "I see Jesus sitting beside you". He also said I have been watching you all the way home, and I couldn't believe what I was seeing! After my mother's funeral, I went back to Washington State and while visiting another friend of mines church for service I went up for prayer.

My friend is a Prophet and she started to lay hands on me, and stepped back. She told the congregation she couldn't pray for me because the angels were around me ministering to me. Also as I was sitting in my living room crocheting, I looked over my shoulder and saw Jesus standing there watching me again.

I had planned an international prayer conference and some things were not going right. Those who were supposed to help didn't, but we prayed and in that conference the Holy Spirit showed up and met us there. One of my friends and some beautiful people from Kenya were so awesome. They helped out with the conference and danced prophetically to the Lord which brought the anointing into the house. My clothing was blowing like there was wind in the room and a quiet, hushed peace came over the room. We knew without a doubt-Jesus was there. (He's So Real)

My latest encounter was in my current home where Jesus came to visit me face-to-face. I saw Him as I was sleeping and woke up to see Him hoovering over me, and He touched me and prayed. I must tell you my God is real. I didn't know much about Him, but He taught me about who He is, and put me around people who taught me about who I am, and more about Him. Despite the bad experiences I have had in life, there has also been some good.

God has taught me so many things, and I thank Him for the intimacy we have, and the anointing He has given me. I pray to use it for His glory and to help others as I surrender to God and step out now to fulfill my purpose and do His will. I am a change-agent, and was born for this time, and so are you. Shalom.

A Prophetic Eagle Released

Going through the storms of being rejected, doors being closed on you, being lied on, and excluded out of the wondrous ministerial groups, being disrespected, offended, and being passed over for positions, and contending with those who think and say "oops" you're not ready or qualified… has been a maturing experience.

After the leader feels they are embarrassed by you, or you don't have the right clothing, don't look the part, or use the right grammar; for you are definitely not the *perfect one* that their God would choose. You are not the *perfect one* whom they were expecting their helper to be, and you just don't fit in and they are not certain where to put you. Hmm, after all of that **"STAND!!!."**

Let your enemies know you are not desperate: for the Bible says, "Be anxious for nothing…" Therefore, "Shake the dust off your feet," and walk away and don't look back. Take bigger steps towards God for He has the master plan for your life, not man. He definitely has a purpose for you, find out what it is and keep it moving. Hold your head up and run like the wind. Be like the eagle who has a broken wing. Take the time to heal, and regain your confidence again. Gather new insight, new vision, and come forth!

Rise up, mount up, and prepare to take flight! Grow in knowledge in the process, let wisdom be your friend, and develop a beautiful, intimate relationship with the King. Become a disciplined soldier, don't accept the scrap bits of man. Keep going, you will see the runway is there and being cleared for you. God will renew your strength, and make your feet like "hinds feet". In spite of what they say, how they try to stop you or block you, it's God giving you a chance. A chance they can't compete with, a chance they can't defeat. It doesn't matter what "witchcraft" they try it is God who will prevail. Ce Ce Winan has a song that says, "You are the way when there seems to be no way. God you have the final say…"

Today, you see a miracle before your eyes, a miracle of faith, a miracle of change, a miracle of life. God has *always* been there even at times when I thought He wasn't. Each time, He has come through for me and to my rescue, and taken care of me and my family. He has communicated with me and taken me to the tops of the mountain, and taught me how to fly. He has repaired my wings, gave me an eagle's insight and discernment, and strengthened my body and inner being. He has prepared me for take off.

I don't think of the challenges and snares from the past, for I barely and faintly remember any hurts at all. With my chest sticking out and my head held high God gives me the signal from heaven, and says "Mount up, spread your wings, let's fly." I hear the sound of angels singing, and the sweet aroma of heaven which permeates the sky, for the launch pad is ready, there's an Eagle in the sky I'm flying past the stratosphere, through the celestial skies. His strength and presence are with me, Hallelujah, I'm on my way!

For I am anointed, appointed, and a majestic "Eagle" with a divine assignment in my hands doing the will of my Father. All Glory and Honor go to Him for He has made me a gift to man from His hands. Amen

Epilogue

In conclusion, it appears there are quite a few hidden things in ministry, which is why this book is entitled "Cloakes of Ministry". It is not just for victims and survivors of abuse but for the knowledge of everyone because speaking out and having a voice could save a life or prevent abuse. It is to make you aware of the red flags in ministry and the difference between toxic and successful ministries.

As we can see, abuse in ministry has been around for decades, and it occurs in the wealthiest to the poorest of cultures. It is up to us to sound the alarm and to bring awareness to this behavior in ministry among leaders, staff, and volunteers. Too many people have been hurt and become victims of this behavior, which definitely must be addressed. Being silent does not help this situation but only harms the victims and survivors more.

Some leaders are disciplined and jailed, while others remain in their clergy positions to continue their bad behavior. Many of these leaders, perhaps, could benefit from mental health therapy, and definitely the victims and survivors. Prayer is not enough, but it takes everyone to do a check and balance to address, monitor, and pay attention to the hidden things in ministry that could harm, whether it be sexual abuse, financial abuse, gossiping, or helping others in the ministry.

The horrors of "Cloaking In Ministry" which is the hidden or disguised things can be harmful, devastating, shameful, and cruel. There are things that can be put in place to help prevent these concealed secret maneuvers done in ministry and the church.

God is definitely unveiling the church and bringing light to what is occurring. It is left up to us as a whole to stand up and help fight this in our churches and bring healing to those who have experienced it. We must recognize the signs, realize everyone cannot lead, and know the difference.

Not many of you should become teachers, my fellow believers, because you know that we who teach will be judged more strictly." James 3:1

CITATIONS

HTTP://brainyquote.com/quotes/robin_s_sharma_628729

John Smithson, Benetta Adamson, July 27, 1994. Children of God, Great Percy Productions. (TV Movie) -mIMDb.

Julia Baird and Hayley Gleeson. Illustration by Rocco Fazzari. (Updated Fri 24 Nov, 10:33 AM AEDT). Raped, tracked, humiliated: Clergy wives speak out about domestic violence. ABC News.- mobile. abc.net.au (2017

Kate Shell nut, May 21, 2019 10:00 AM. 1 in 10 Young Protestants Have Left a Church Over Abuse. Http://www.christianitytoday.com.

King James Version Bible Standard Edition (1930/2013), Christian Art Publishers & The Livingstone Corporation.

Lisa Miller, September 23, 2019, Foreign Correspondent, The 'hidden children' of the Catholic church are refusing to live in secrecy anymore..

Martin Sixsmith, June 8, 2014 https://www.dailymail.co.uk.news (Special report) I found nuns' secret grave for 800 babies in Tuam.

Myles Monroe, 2001.Understanding the Purpose and Power of Women. God's Design For Female Identity. Expanded Edition With Study Guide. Whitaker House

Rebekah Drumsta, Christianity.com,September 2022. What is the Meaning and significance of Redeemption?

Robin S. Dharma. Quotes. (n.d.). BrainyQuote.com. Retrieved March 1, 2022, from Brainstorming.

Sophia Tewa, Sat 11 March 2017 04:00 EST. The Guardian, Religion, Life after a sex cult: 'If I'm not a member of this religion any more, then who am I?'

Made in the USA
Las Vegas, NV
18 October 2023

79211844R00056